I0765523

I hope life treats you kind

And I hope you have all you have dreamed of

And I wish you joy and happiness

But above all this I wish you love!

Date:

Nº 543.

Date:

Date:

Date:

Date:

Date:

Date:

Date:

Date:

Date:

Date:

Date:

Date:

Date:
Date:

Date:

P. Préval

Date:

Anaïs Toudouze

Date:

Anais Toudouze

Date:

Tetquin fils, imp. Paris.

Date:

Réville Imp. r. St Victor 55 à Paris

Date:

Date:

Date:

Laure Noël

Date:

Date:

Date:

Date:

Reproduction interdite

Date:

Date:

Lerey imp Paris

Date:

Leroy. imp. Paris
Anaïs Coudouze

Date:

Date:

Date:

Date:

Falconer imp. Paris

Date:

Reproduction interdite

Date:

Reproduction interdite

Date:

Date:

Delsgrange

Date:

Date:

Date:

Date:

Hardcover ISBN 978-1-7750654-2-5

Summary: Victorian Wedding Guest Book. Featuring 40 full colour fashion plates from
various French, Brithish and Italian fashion periodicals published between the 1840's
and 1880's.

Designed in Canada ; Printed and bound in USA.